Sadi Thread & Shisha
Glass Embroidery

Sadi Thread & Shisha Glass Embroidery

Betty Luke

SALLY MILNER PUBLISHING

First published in 2001 by
Sally Milner Publishing Pty Ltd
PO Box 2104
Bowral NSW 2576
AUSTRALIA

Design Ken Gilroy
Editing Lyneve Rappell
Photography Richard Gibbs

Printed in Hong Kong

National Library of Australia
Cataloguing-in-Publication data:
Luke, Elizabeth E.
  Sadi thread and shisha glass embroidery

  ISBN 1 86351 265 9

  1. Shisha mirror embroidery. 2. Embroidery. I. Title.
746.44

Sections of this book are reproduced by permission of
Louise Howland.

Disclaimer
The information in this instruction book is presented in good
faith. However, no warranty is given, nor results guaranteed, nor
is freedom from any patent to be inferred. Since we have no
control over the use of information contained in this book, the
publisher and the author disclaim liability for untoward results.

Dedication To Bill
For his love,
support and
sense of humour.

Foreword

Sadi thread and Shisha glass have long been a source of fascination for me. Sharing ideas for their application has occupied much of my time for the past decade. It is always exciting for me to see what talented and creative embroiderers choose to do with these media.

Betty Luke is a woman of immense knowledge, creative thinking and excellent teaching skills, wonderfully combined with great patience and humour. Her exploration of the possibilities of applications for sadi and shisha has led to the creation of the many diverse designs in this book. The artistic versatility demonstrated here will, I'm sure, inspire every stitcher who sees Betty's work to extend their style.

As stitchers, I think we all seek to create beauty and to leave something of our individual character on the work we do. Enjoyment is to be had at every stage: from the design planning; the collection of materials; the stitching and finishing; to finally, the satisfaction felt on completion when our embroidery, be it great or small, reaches its destination. Sadi and Shisha give special pleasure at each stage. They can impart infinite variety with a little practice and the use of imagination.

The designs here are meant to be both instructional and inspirational. Betty shares with you elemental techniques for applying sadi and shisha, and provides designs that put these techniques into practice. These designs may be applied to a variety of articles of your choice, whether clothing, evening or wedding apparel, wearable accessories, jewellery, pictures, book covers, boxes, home articles such as cushion covers, curtain tie-backs, table linens and decorations.

May you take pleasure in developing your own variations and style from the basics provided here. I wish you very many happy hours of stitching.

Louise Howland

Sadi & Shisha # Contents

Introduction   10

Materials   12

Techniques   17

Projects

   Laid Sadi Posy   28

   Sadi Borders   32

      • Floral Border   32

      • Feather Flower Border   33

      • Spring Flower Border   35

   Three Leaves in Gold   36

   The Purple Shaded Leaf   38

   Silk Feather   39

   The Brolga   40

   The Ladybird, Bumble Bee & Dragonfly   43

   Sadi & Shisha 'R'   47

   A Sadi Sampler   49

   Silhouette of a Rose   52

   The Fairies' Shisha Tree   54

   Shisha with Covered Washers   59

   Shisha Tortoise   61

   Blue Diamond Flower   64

   Golden Wattle   67

   Sadi Wallflowers   70

   The Strawberry Plant   74

   Raised Pink Bell Flowers   79

   Silvery Moon Owl   83

Stitch Guide   88

Betty Luke   94

Suppliers   95

Introduction

The place of Sadi Threads and Shisha (mirror) Glass in different embroidery styles could fill a number of books! There is enormous scope for experimentation in all aspects of these distinctive materials in your needlework.

Sadi Thread

Sadi (sometimes called 'purl') thread is made of fine wire coiled into a hollow spring. It is tubular and flexible so it can be formed into curves, spirals, twists and scrolls to decorate fabrics from suede to silk, moiré to mohair. It has an ancient tradition, and has long been a vital element in the sumptuous decorations on regal, ecclesiastical, military and other ceremonial garments and accessories.

The use of silver and gold for robes and cloths is mentioned in both the Iliad and the Odyssey; the ancient Egyptians also decorated special garments with gold threads. Archaeological records demonstrate the sophisticated working of metal threads from the early Byzantine period. Threads of beaten wire are mentioned in the Bible, where they were used to decorate robes. The fortunate Aaron had an ephod (a surplice worn by a Jewish priest) of gold, blue, purple and scarlet, decorated with gold beaten into plates then cut into wires and worked (Exodus 39:2-3). Indeed, the method of manufacture of sadi thread has changed little since biblical times.

Sadi has been somewhat neglected in recent years, but it is still very capable of adding brilliance to embroideries, whether they be simple or complex, amateur or professional. Sadi can make itself at home in many places: as bullion in wool embroidery; as beads covering an exotic gown; as a vital element of goldwork; or simply enhancing long stitch. Couching sadi into various patterns, grouping together different types of sadi and padding the work to add dimension, can create a variety of effects.

Raised work is one of the numerous homes in which sadi feels immensely comfortable. It was particularly well suited to the raised embroidery of Elizabethan times, in which plaited gold stems were raised from fabrics. Petals, leaves and suchlike – often padded with lamb's wool or horsehair and worked in detached buttonhole stitch, sometimes over a wire framework so that they stood away from the background in relief – relied on sadi to provide the richness desired. Several examples of raised work appear towards the end of this book.

Shisha (Mirror) Glass

The history of shisha (mirror) glass is also fascinating. Shisha has been used in embroidery since glass was invented. Even before glass, materials with light reflective qualities were used as decoration.

An integral part of the folk embroidery of Russia and central Asia for many centuries, traditional shisha is believed to have originated from north-west India. The wealthy classes of central Asia, Russia and the Indian subcontinent wore clothing embroidered with precious metal threads and jewels.

Camel girths and various other animal decorations were (and still are) embroidered using coloured silks, metal threads and shisha. Less prosperous people used cheaper decorations, like chips of mica and beetle's wings embroidered onto cloth, to give a rich, luxurious look. During the 1500s, mica and wings were largely replaced by pieces of mirror.

In the 1600s, shisha replaced mica in the beautiful stumpwork of Stuart times. Embroiderers began attaching mirrors to all sorts of garments and cloth. The most prevalent motifs and designs have been stylised plants, animals and geometric forms.

To this day shisha work is part of the great embroidery traditions of many Eastern countries, and is once again reaching into Western embroidery, adding exciting dimensions to raised embroidery designs and applications both traditional and innovative. Shisha provides a charming and inexpensive way to add interest and beauty to many different embroidery styles.

Shisha may be applied to a variety of designs on clothing, box lids, sleeves, bags, cushion covers, cummerbunds, decorations, purses, drawstring bags, jackets, placemats, napkins, tablecloths, wall hangings, book covers, caps, waistcoats, yokes, scarves and quilts.

Materials

Frame

A frame is essential for all sadi and shisha work, otherwise stitching tends to pucker the fabric. Damp stretching is not possible for metal embroidery so it is important that the fabric is kept taut during stitching. A hands-free table, slate or floor frame is ideal, as it means you can use both hands to embroider while keeping even tension on the fabric. It also allows you to see all of your design at once.

A ring frame or hoop is adequate for small designs although it does not have the advantage of giving you a spare hand. Tightly wrap a length of cotton tape around the inner ring of the hoop to prevent damage to fine fabrics. One major drawback of a ring frame for larger designs is that if you need to move the frame to stitch another area you may damage the work you have done.

Muslin or tissue paper may be tacked over the worked areas to protect the embroidery from dust, hand contact and prevent working threads catching on the finished area.

Fabric

Virtually any fabric can be used for this type of work! Dress, furnishing and specialist embroidery fabrics provide enormous choices. Consider the design, the stitching techniques, colours, materials (including weight) and the finished purpose of the embroidery whilst pondering the choices. The choice of fabric is largely personal.

Silk reflects the luminosity of the metals and mirrors, a matt or slub is a wonderful contrast. A firm fabric is preferable; however, lighter and loosely woven fabrics are perfect, provided you back them. Backing gives the fabric body and prevents puckering thereby improving the finished appearance of the embroidery.

If you wish to frame your finished embroidery, allow at least 4 in (10 cm) additional fabric to allow for tensioning of the fabric prior to framing. Depending on the type of embroidery hoop or embroidery frame you are working with, the margin may need to be even greater.

Backing

The embroideries in this book have all had a fine cotton self-adhesive backing ironed to the wrong side of the fabric prior to stitching, but medium-weight linen or pre-shrunk calico are also good backing materials.

Tracing Paper

Use this to trace the designs in this book. White kitchen paper works well.

Transfer Paper

Transfer paper is similar to dressmaker's carbon and does not smudge. Use it, between the traced design and the back of the fabric, to transfer the design.

HB Pencil

A sharp HB pencil is used to trace the design onto tracing paper, and to transfer the design to the fabric via the transfer paper.

Needles

Please refer to this needle guide whilst stitching.

The type of needle depends on the technique you are using.

Crewel 6-8 for working with more than two strands of thread.

Crewel 8-10 for working with one or two strands of thread.

Straw 7-9 for sadi beading, sadi bullions, and knot stitches. Needle points are very useful for picking up sadi beads.

Chenille 18-22 for stitching with Rajcord, plunging sadi and cake wire ends.

Tapestry 20-26 for stitching over previously worked areas and for needleweaving. The blunt point will slip between threads without splitting them.

Rajmahal Art Silk Threads

Art Silks can be used anywhere that you would use stranded cotton, but they give a special finish to embroidery designs. Art Silks are less likely to 'catch' on sadi than other threads are, and they reflect light beautifully in both sadi and shisha embroidery.

As Art Silks are stranded (six strands each of 8 metres), they may be separated and recombined, so that the thickness of the thread may be altered to suit your embroidery. As well as altering the thickness of your thread in this way, you can also achieve a greater colour palette. By 'tweeding' various shades (combining different colours in the needle) you will be able to create effects like subtle tone gradations.

Always wind your Art Silks onto a card before use, and write the thread number on the card. Thread your needle from the spool and then cut the thread so that you always work with the grain of the thread rather than against it. If using more than one strand of thread, separate the strands and then put them together again. This will give you a smoother surface to your stitching.

Rajmahal Metal Threads

Reflecting and directing the play of light is the essential powerful element in sadi and shisha work. The sewing threads must suit! Rajmahal metal threads are ideal. When stitching with either the Hand Sew or Machine Metal (the latter is stronger) always keep the thread taut, and occasionally renew the twist by rolling the needle between your fingers.

Beeswax

Smooth and strengthen Art Silk threads and metal threads by running them through beeswax prior to use. Threads that are used to pass through or couch sadi, and threads used to attach shisha, should be waxed.

Rajmahal Sadi Threads

Rajmahal sadi threads are either gold or silver and come in smooth, check (faceted) and pearl (tighter coils with less 'stretch' and a beaded appearance) finishes. They are packaged in clear tubes with a screw lid, and the quantity in each container depends on the type. Always store sadi in an airtight container in a cool and dark place. If wrapping, use acid-free tissue paper.

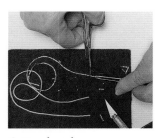

Cutting board

Cutting Board

A cutting board of approximately 6" x 4" (15 x 10 cm) is adequate for most work.

A felt covered board is preferable to prevent sadi from 'jumping' when it is cut. It is quite simple to make one by simply gluing felt (dark green is best) to strong cardboard. When the glue is dry, cut the felt flush with the card.

Scissors

Keep a pair of strong scissors with straight long points for cutting metal threads only. Alternatively, a scalpel is excellent for cutting sadi lengths. Place the length of sadi on the cutting board, and make a deft cut with the scalpel or scissors exactly at right angles to the thread. You will also require separate scissors for cutting Art Silk thread.

Forceps or Tweezers

Small dressing forceps or tweezers are used for positioning sadi and minimising handling.

Rajmahal Shisha (Mirror) Glass

Rajmahal Shisha (Mirror) Glass is available in small and large sizes of round or diamond-shaped pieces. The pieces come packaged in clear tubes with a screw-on lid. The number of pieces per tube depends on the size of the shisha, e.g. 30 small round shisha are contained in one tube.

Honing stone

Honing Stone

Also known as an oilstone, this is important for smoothing the edges of the shisha prior to use (available at hardware stores).

Washers

These are used for attaching shisha pieces by the Covered Ring Method (see Techniques). Take the pieces of shisha to a hardware, plumbing or curtain store to choose rings or washers that are the correct size (i.e. slightly smaller than the actual mirror). Rings may be flat (like a fibre washer) or rounded.

Tulle

This is used for attaching shisha by the Fabric Cover technique (see Techniques).

Cords

Decorative cords can be purchased or very simply made in your desired thickness and colouring. Cord may be couched, slipstitched or threaded through a chenille needle and worked as a regular thread.

Some excellent effects can be produced by needleweaving, whipping and the use of contrasting Art Silk threads. If whipping or weaving around stitched cord, use a tapestry needle to prevent the needle splitting the cord.

Rajmahal Rajcord is available in both gold and silver, on reels of 35 metres.

Covered Cake Wire 28

For raised work.

Padding

Felt (yellow for gold/pale grey for silver), card, soft cotton cord, pellon, fine batting, leathers, etc. are used for raised embroidery.

Vilene

In some projects, this is used for making slips.

Stiletto

This can be a useful item for opening larger holes in fabric if you wish to plunge sadi or cords through to the wrong side.

Techniques

Design Transfer

There are many ways to transfer a design. The method you choose will depend on the fabric (type and colour) to be stitched, the embroidery style and your personal preference.

Fabric should be placed in a frame, or taped (or pinned) taut to a flat surface, before the design is transferred.

Trace the design onto tracing paper. On the wrong side of the fabric place a sheet of transfer paper. Then lay the tracing paper, with the design back to front, over the transfer paper. With a sharp HB pencil, draw over the design.

With a thread matching the fabric, tack around the design using a Crewel 10 needle. Tacking stitches should be shorter on the right side of the work. This method allows you to alter the design and prevents the right side of the fabric being marked.

When the embroidery is completed, any tacking stitches that are still visible can be easily removed by gently plucking them out with a pair of tweezers.

Attaching Sadi Thread

Handle sadi as little as possible. Rather than touching the metal directly, use tweezers as much as is practical, and work in a pair of latex surgical gloves if you can. Provided they fit 'like a glove', they will not hamper your stitching and will prevent perspiration etc. from coming into contact with the metal.

Note: Once sadi has been stretched it does not recoil!

Couching

A traditional technique to which sadi is well suited. A surprising number of effects can be achieved with this very simple stitch.

Position sadi on the right side of the fabric leaving a tail of about $5/8$" (2 cm). Thread a crewel needle with your working thread (e.g. matching or contrasting, a metal thread or Rajmahal Art Silk). Draw the working thread through beeswax prior to use to prevent friction and ensure strength.

Secure the working thread with two stitches or a knot in the back of the fabric, and bring it to the right side. Take small stitches, approximately $1/4$" (6 mm) apart (this distance depends on the effect desired), at right angles to the sadi. Couching stitches should be firm enough to hold the sadi in place but not so tight as to cause the sadi to kink.

Pearl sadi is best for couching when sharp angles are required but all sadi threads are pliable enough to bend at sharp angles. Secure any corner with one stitch. If couching double lines of sadi, the corners or angles are handled a little differently in that the outer sadi thread is couched first with a diagonal stitch, then the inner line of sadi is couched likewise. When both lines of sadi face the new direction they can be couched as paired threads once more.

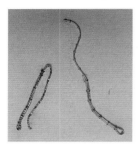

The two main threads

The coils of pearl sadi may be gently stretched a little, so that the working thread slips between the coils. If you are couching with this method, make sure that your first stitch slips into the first coil.

'Stroking' the sadi gently into shape is important when working curves.

To fill a shape with couched sadi, always begin from the outside of the shape. This establishes the outline correctly.

To finish, sadi ends may be cut flush and remain on top of the work. The ends are stitched over firmly. Experienced stitchers may prefer to plunge sadi ends.

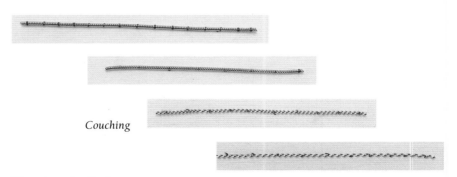

Couching

Plunging the Ends

Please practise this method before attempting it on finished embroidery. Plunging involves making a hole in the fabric with a stiletto, then threading the sadi through a large eyed chenille needle and taking it through the hole to the wrong side of the fabric. Secure the sadi on the wrong side by oversewing. Before oversewing, gently stretch the sadi to spread out the coils rather than have a lump! Note: Smooth and pearl sadi are more difficult to plunge than check sadi.

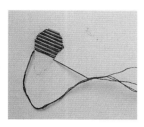

Laid technique

Laid Technique

Stitch fine parallel guidelines across your pattern using one strand of thread.

Take a length of sadi, hold it along the first line and kink it with scissor tips to mark the length required. Cut the sadi to this length.

Thread a straw needle with two strands of waxed thread. Bring the needle up through the reverse side of the fabric, at one end of the line along which the sadi will be laid. Pick up the sadi with the point of the needle, and then pass the needle and thread through the centre of the sadi (as one would thread a bead).

Bring the needle down at the other end of the line, so that the sadi lies flat. Take the needle through to the reverse of the fabric. Note that the sadi itself is not pulled through to wrong side, only the thread. Long stitches of thread may be alternated with the lines of sadi.

Sadi Lazy Daisy

Using one strand of metal thread and a Crewel 7 needle, bring the needle through to the right side of the fabric. Thread on a length of sadi then pass the needle back into the point where the thread emerges from the fabric. This causes the sadi to

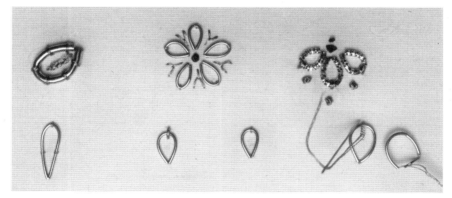

Sadi Lazy Daisy

form a loop. Stitch the loop to the fabric with a small straight stitch. The straight stitch may or may not have a piece of sadi threaded onto it, depending on the desired effect.

Sadi Bullion

A wonderful dimension can be added to bullions by incorporating sadi thread. The sizes and types of sadi used may be altered as desired.

Work three, six-wrap bullion stitches with Rajmahal Art Silk thread to form the centre of the rose. Bring the thread though at 1.

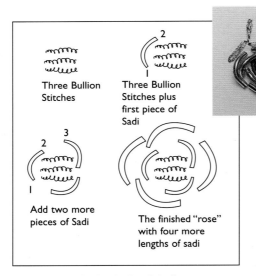

Three Bullion Stitches

Three Bullion Stitches plus first piece of Sadi

Add two more pieces of Sadi

The finished "rose" with four more lengths of sadi

An example of a finished Sadi bullion rose

Thread a $^3/_{16}$" (5 mm) length of sadi onto the straw needle (as one would thread on a bead) then take the needle through the fabric at 2. Bring the needle out at 3, drawing the thread through the fabric firmly. One at a time, position two $^3/_{16}$" (5 mm) lengths of sadi, to complete the inner circle (see drawing).

Bring the needle out $^1/_8$" (3 mm) from the end of the last piece of sadi from the reverse side, so that the sadi ends can be tucked under. Work four more lengths of $^3/_{16}$" (5mm) sadi closely around the inner circle using the same method.

Padding

Felt can be used to raise the sadi from the background. One, two or more layers of felt may be used. Starting with the smallest size, and in the centre of the area, stab stitch the felt into place.

Felt or detached buttonhole stitch areas (as in the Strawberry Design) can be padded with Fibre Fill. It is always important not to overfill as this can distort the background fabric.

Padding and Sadi Beading techniques

Cords can be couched to the background and sadi or Rajcord couched over the top. This produces a rippled effect. Burden stitch falls into this category.

Sadi Beading

Sadi may be cut into shorter lengths and sewn down – as one would sew a bead – in a variety of ways. The flexibility of sadi means that the bead lengths can be curved if desired. Sadi can be made to stand up from the fabric in 'loops' simply by securing a longer length of sadi with a shorter stitch.

Glue

PVA glue can be used to attach sadi.

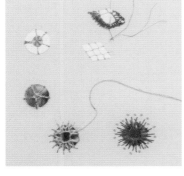

Attaching Shisha glass

Attaching Shisha (Mirror) Glass

Take care when handling shisha! The pieces are hand cut, and the edges can be sharp. It is imperative that you smooth the edges (using a honing stone or oilstone) before stitching, or the glass may cut through the thread.

There are no holes drilled in shisha, and they cannot be pierced. The pieces are held in place by a framework of embroidery. Once the basic frame stitches are mastered, endless stitch and thread combinations can be used to embellish the frame.

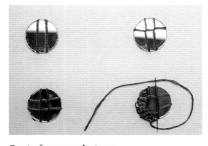

Basic frame technique

Basic Shisha Frame

Mark the fabric to show where the shisha will be placed. Secure a thread or cord with a knot on the right side and then place the mirror over the knot. Holding the shisha between your thumb and index finger, stitch two parallel, vertical long stitches (12 o'clock to 6 o'clock) across the glass. Take a small backstitch to secure the thread and then stitch two parallel, horizontal long stitches at right angles to the first pair (9 o'clock to 3 o'clock). Rather than making the horizontal stitches go straight across the mirror, hook each one over and under each of the vertical stitches. Take a backstitch to secure the frame.

The shisha is stable if only the basic frame is applied. If desired, a further set of frame stitches may be laid diagonally over the first square to form an octagon in the centre.

The tension of the basic frame stitches is important because the frame will be pulled out towards the edge of the mirror by additional decorative stitches. If it is too loose the mirror may fall out of the stitched frame; too tight and the stitching will be difficult to pull out from the centre, leaving the mirror hidden.

Decorating the Basic Frame

To decorate the frame, bring the decorative thread to the right side of the fabric, and incorporate your decorative stitches by attaching them to the centre of frame. The decorative thread may go under then over the frame, or over then under, depending on the stitch you are using and effect you wish to produce. Buttonhole stitch, twisted chain stitch, French knots and Cretan stitch are commonly used.

Sadi Thread Frame

Sadi may be threaded onto Art Silk (using a Straw 7 needle) and laid across shisha to form a decorative feature on the front of the shisha. Do not attempt to pull the sadi through the fabric. Only the working thread pierces the fabric. Measure and cut the lengths of sadi before stitching.

Covered Ring Frame

Buttonhole stitch or crotchet around the ring or washer in Rajmahal Art Silk thread, Rajmahal Rajcord or metal thread. Then simply place the ring over the mirror, and slip-stitch the covered ring into place from the wrong side.

Covered Ring frame

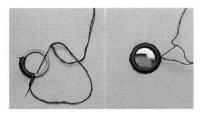

Fabric Cover

Shisha may be attached by applying a 'looking-glass' cover of sheer fabric, e.g. tulle, muslin, chiffon, etc. Cut the fabric slightly larger than the shisha. Then, holding the shisha in place, embroider the edge of the covering fabric to your main fabric using the stitches and threads of your choice. Mirrors can also be decorated with surrounding concentric patterns of stitching, making the mirror a central feature from which to expand your design.

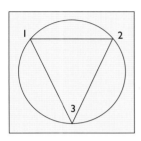

Triangle Shisha frame

Triangle Shisha frame

Come up at one, down at two, up at three, down at one, up at three, down at two.

Five Spoke Foundation

As the five spoke foundation must be firm enough to hold a spider web of needleweaving, use five or six strands of thread or a length of Rajmahal Rajcord.

Anchor your thread with a knot on the right side of the fabric or small backstitches on the wrong side. Hold the shisha over the anchoring knot.

Bring the needle up at 1, down at 2 (do not pull the thread through, leave a loop).

Come up at 3. Take the needle over and under the loop. Adjust the threads to the centre of the shisha. Repeat the 'over and under' again. Take the needle down at 4. Work a small backstitch close to the edge of the shisha.

Five spoke foundation

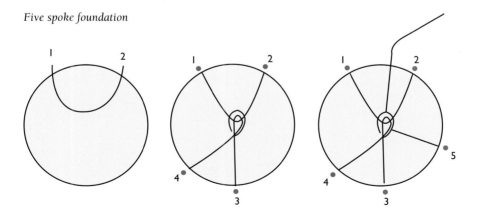

Come up at 5, then over and under the central area twice. The thread can now be taken down through 1 and finished under the shisha or used for needleweaving. It may be used straight away or laid to one side to be used later for weaving.

Eight Spoke Foundation

After securing your thread, create the eight spokes by bringing the needle up on the uneven numbers and down on the even numbers. Finish off under the shisha.

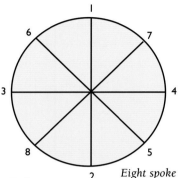

Eight spoke foundation

Securing the Thread for Needleweaving

This applies to both the Five and the Eight Spoke Foundations. To join in a new thread to commence needleweaving a spider web decoration, place a knot right at the end of a thread and bring the needle up from under the centre of the spokes. As you weave, all signs of the knot will disappear. To finish, secure the thread with a few small stitches, under the threads, at the point where the spokes meet.

1

2

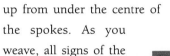

3

4

5

6

Machine Application

It is also possible to attached shisha using a free machine featherstitch. Make sure that the needle pierces the fabric very close to the edge of the shisha. Have the bobbin tension much looser than the needle thread tension so that long loops form over the shisha.

Glue

PVA glue can also be used to attach the shisha pieces.

Cleaning

Metal threads should never be immersed in water. Surface dirt can be removed by sprinkling magnesium carbonate (a pharmaceutical product) thinly on the fabric surface and leaving it for a few minutes. Remove it with a soft brush or by covering a vacuum cleaner nozzle with fine nylon net and vacuuming, on a low setting, in circular movements, over the surface of the fabric.

Finishing

Turn to the wrong side of your embroidery. Trim all the ends to about $^4/_{10}$ in (1 cm), gently stretching any sadi thread that may form a lump. Ends should lie under a worked area of embroidery, if at all possible, to prevent a bumpy front view.

Press the work from the wrong side with a suitably hot iron for your fabric. If possible, keep the work in the embroidery frame if the piece is going to be framed. Don't iron directly on the metal threads or shisha, or press too hard with the iron.

Work is then ready for making up or mounting. If your embroidery is to be a framed, I recommend a frame with glass, as it is one of the best ways to prevent the discolouration of threads.

The Projects

Laid Sadi Posy

Mastering this very simple technique means that you can create original and fulfilling designs with utmost ease.

Materials
Rajmahal Art Silk 133, 202, 742.
Rajmahal Silver Metal Thread
Rajmahal Rajcord (silver)
Rajmahal Smooth Sadi Thread (silver)
Needle: Crewel 9

Techniques
Couching, laid sadi.

Stitches
Couching, French knots, straight stitch.

Method
Prepare the fabric and transfer the design as usual.

Commence with the stems. Double a piece of Rajcord. Then, starting at the base of the stem, use the metal thread to couch the doubled Rajcord up to the fork, where the stem branches out to each flower.

Cut and couch a separate, single piece of cord for the stem leading to the bud.

The flowers are filled with alternate rows of laid sadi followed by a long straight stitch. To begin the first stitch, thread a length of smooth sadi which has been pre-cut to the length of the line. The second stitch is a long straight stitch in the same thread. Alternate a long stitch with a piece of laid sadi to continue the pattern.

The upper flower has five strands of 202 in the four top petals. The lower petals have two strands of 202 and three strands of 742 combined in one needle.

The lower flower has three petals worked with five strands of 742. The lower petal and the petal closest to the stem are worked in two strands of 742 and three strands of 202 combined in one needle.

The flower centres are French knots worked in six strands of 202.

Leaves are worked with four strands of 133.

The bud is worked in four strands of 742.

Minimum effort and maximum effect can be gained by mastering this very simple technique. Designing is as simple as drawing shapes and stitching parallel lines. Varying the number of satin stitches taken between the Sadi, varying the type of Sadi, varying the direction of the lines and shapes, adding Shisha, Sadi bullions, beads, sequins for centres will mean that you can create original and fulfilling designs with utmost ease.

Sadi Borders

Using simple techniques and superb materials, you can adapt these borders to feature on evening wear and accessories, curtain tie backs, panels, table linen, book covers, box lids, etc. Border designs can be taken out of this context and rearranged into squares, diagonals, and trellises. Part of the border can be centred to form a motif if so desired.

Floral Border

Materials
Rajmahal Art Silk 379, 421.
Rajmahal Gold Metal Thread
Rajmahal Rajcord (gold)
Rajmahal Pearl Sadi Thread (gold)
Rajmahal Broad Check Sadi Thread (gold)
Needles: Straw 7; Crewel 7, 9.

Techniques
Couching

Stitches
Couching, stem stitch.

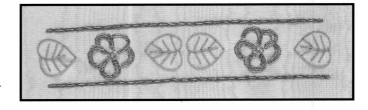

Method
Prepare the fabric and transfer the design as usual.

The outside two rows are worked in stem stitch using six strands of 379. Six strands of 421 are then couched between the stem stitch rows, using one strand of gold metal thread.

The leaves are pearl sadi couched with gold metal thread.

The flowers are three rows of Rajcord couched with gold metal thread. Each flower centre is a length of broad check sadi couched into a small circle using gold metal thread.

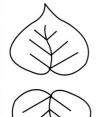

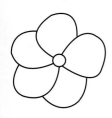

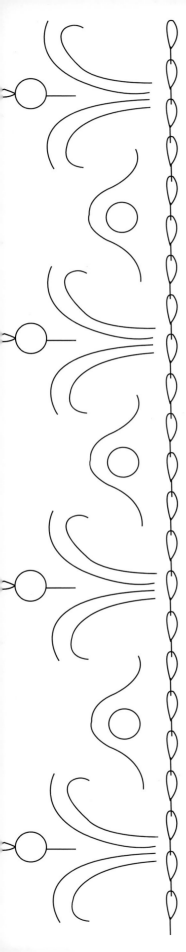

Feather Flower Border

Materials

Rajmahal Art Silk Thread 251, 255.
Rajmahal Silver Metal Thread
Rajmahal Rajcord (silver)
Rajmahal Smooth Sadi Thread (silver)
Rajmahal Check Sadi Thread (silver)
Rajmahal Pearl Sadi Thread (silver)
Rajmahal Shisha (Mirror) Glass (small round)
Needles: Straw 7; Crewel 8.

Techniques

Couching, shisha basic frame, sadi lazy daisy, laid sadi.

Stitches

Buttonhole, couching.

Method

Prepare the fabric and transfer the design as usual.

The shisha pieces are attached by a basic shisha frame with a buttonhole edge. The flower piece is worked with three strands of 255. The piece that forms the 'eye' of the hill is applied using three strands of 251.

The lower edge is a 'Fob Chain'. It consists of loops of smooth sadi attached lazy daisy style, with each daisy petal connected with a straight laid length of check sadi.

A curving 'hill' of pearl sadi is couched with metal thread.

The leaves are Rajcord couched with metal thread.

The flower stem is a laid length of smooth sadi.

The shisha flower is capped with a lazy daisy loop of check sadi, stitched at the apex with six strands of 255.

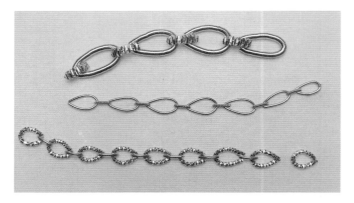

Fob chain stitches

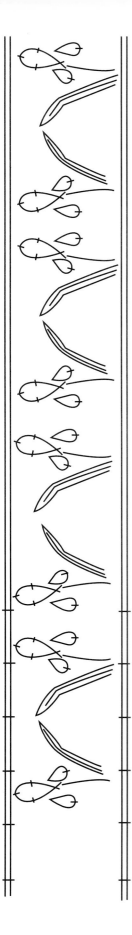

Spring Flower Border

Materials

Rajmahal Silver Metal Thread

Rajmahal Rajcord (silver)

Rajmahal Smooth Sadi Thread (silver)

Rajmahal Pearl Sadi Thread (silver)

Needles: Straw 7; Crewel 9.

Techniques

Sadi lazy daisy, couching.

Stitches

Couching, straight stitch.

Method

Prepare the fabric and transfer the design as usual.

The outside lines are doubled lengths of Rajcord couched together using metal thread.

The leaves are straight stitches worked in two strands of metal thread.

The stalks are pearl sadi couched with one strand of metal thread.

The petals are smooth sadi attached using the Lazy Daisy techniques, held with one strand of metal thread. The larger central petal is formed to appear as a twisted chain stitch, whilst the lower petals are as lazy daisies.

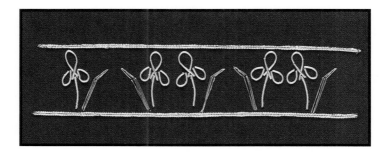

Three Leaves in Gold

Materials

Rajmahal Gold Metal Thread

Rajmahal Rajcord (gold)

Rajmahal Pearl Sadi Thread (gold)

Rajmahal Smooth Sadi Thread (gold)

Rajmahal Check Sadi Thread (gold)

Rajmahal Broad Check Sadi Thread (gold)

Rajmahal Broad Smooth Sadi Thread (gold)

Needles: Crewel 9; Straw 8.

Techniques

Laid sadi, couching, sadi beading.

Stitches

Couching.

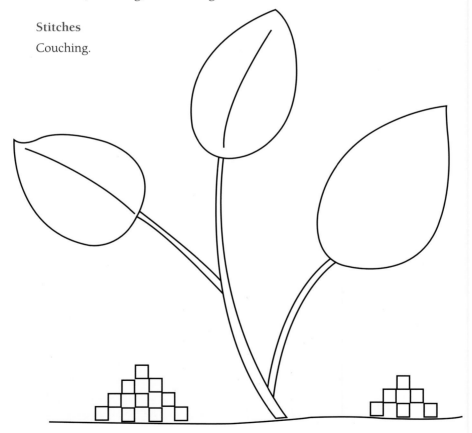

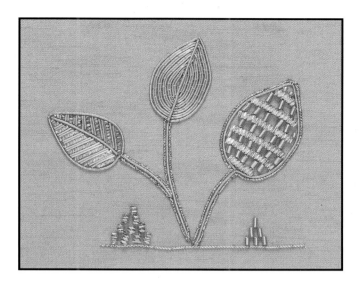

Method

Prepare the fabric and transfer the design as usual.

Metal thread has been used as the couching thread throughout this embroidery.

Leaf 1. The central vein is couched pearl sadi. The leaf has alternate rows of two smooth sadi and one check sadi laid using metal thread. The sadi is worked in the direction of leaf veins. The leaf is outlined with couched pearl sadi.

Leaf 2 - features smooth sadi. Pairs of lines of smooth sadi thread are couched as one (i.e. together). The central vein of pearl sadi is couched. This is couched after the smooth sadi has been worked. The outline is couched pearl sadi.

Leaf 3 - has bands of broad check sadi and broad smooth sadi. The outline is pearl sadi, which is in turn outlined with one strand of couched Rajcord.

The stems are all of pearl sadi with Rajcord on each side.

The left-hand blocks are ten pieces of broad check sadi, stitched down using the bead technique.

The right hand blocks are six pieces of broad smooth sadi stitched down using the bead technique.

The design sits on a line of couched pulled (stretched) pearl sadi.

The couchng thread is gold metal.

The Purple Shaded Leaf

Materials
Rajmahal Art Silk 111, 113, 115.
Rajmahal Gold Metal Thread
Rajmahal Pearl Sadi Thread (gold)
Needles: Crewel 9

Techniques
Couching

Stitches
Couching, split stitch.

Method
Prepare the background fabric and transfer the design as usual.

Two strands of thread are used for all the shading. The working direction for the split stitch is from the centre of the vein sloping gently upwards. Follow the diagram for the shading combinations.

The centre vein commences with a doubled length of pearl sadi, and finishes with the pearl sadi stretched slightly. The sadi is couched with one strand of gold metal thread.

The side veins are stretched sadi, couched with one strand of metal thread.

Use one strand of each colour in the numbered sections.
Section 1   115+115
2   115+113
3   113+113
4   113+111
5   111+111

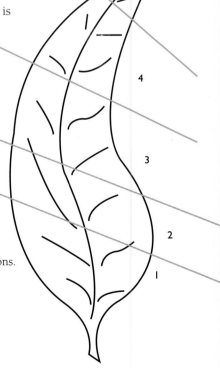

Silk Feather

Materials

Rajmahal Art Silk 121, 122, 126, 221, 226.

Rajmahal Silver Metal Thread

Rajmahal Rajcord (silver)

Needles: Crewel 8

Stitches

Couching, satin stitch.

Method

Prepare the fabric and transfer the design as usual.

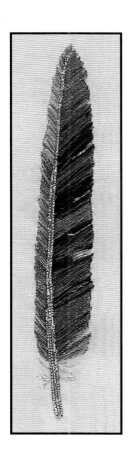

Use three strands of thread throughout the embroidery.

The narrow side of the feather is shaded, in satin stitch, from the tip with 121, 221 and 226. Gradually mix the different coloured strands of thread from dark to light.

The other side of the feather is graded with the blues 121, 122, 126, but mixing the shading down the feather. The lowest section is a single strand of 221. Two strands of silver metal thread are blended in with the blues.

The shaft is Rajcord, starting with three strands and ending with one strand at the tip. The Rajcord is couched with one strand of metal thread. This feather embroidery would make an ideal book mark.

The Brolga

The Brolga is Australia's most elegant dancing bird. Dancing displays of leaps, bows and prancing steps are performed by birds of both sexes. They live in the grasslands at the edge of swamps.

Materials
Rajmahal Art Silk 25, 101,122, 201, 211, 221, 226, 235, 255, 805, 926.
Rajmahal Silver Metal Thread
Rajmahal Pearl Sadi Thread (silver)
Rajmahal Check Sadi Thread (silver)
Needles: Crewel 8, 9.

Techniques
Couching, laid sadi.

Stitches
Backstitch, French knots, couching, Roumanian couching, satin stitch, stem stitch, straight stitch.

Method
Prepare the fabric and transfer the design as usual.

The wings are worked in shaded satin stitch, going from dark grey on the tips to pale grey.

The shading is worked in the following sequence, using one strand of each thread combined in the needle.

25/25/25

25/25/226

25/226/226

226/226/226

226/226/221

226/221/221

221/221/221

Outline the wings with gently stretched pearl sadi as shown in the picture, couched with one strand of metal thread.

The body, neck and head are worked in Roumanian couching using two strands of 201. This gives a feathery look.

The skin behind the eyes is one strand each of 235 and 255 worked with small straight stitches.

The beak is satin stitch in two strands of 226.

The eyes are French knots using two strands of 25.

The legs are one strand each of 226 and 25, combined in the needle. They are long straight stitches, couched with one strand of 226.

Stretched pearl sadi outlines the body, legs and head, as per the picture. The sadi is couched with one strand of metal thread.

One strand of 122 is backstitched across the lower wings and behind the legs. And, one strand of 226 is backstitched along back of neck, body and under head.

The water is in stem stitch, using two strands each of 211 and 101.

The reeds are two strands of 805 in Romanian couching and straight stitches, tipped with check sadi.

The distant reeds are: a) two strands of 926; and, b) one strand each of 926 and 101.

The Ladybird, Bumble Bee & Dragonfly

Insects always add interest to embroideries, whether they are the main feature or in the background.

Materials
Rajmahal Art Silk 25, 29, 93, 101, 175, 235, 225, 226, 255, 311, 805.
Rajmahal Gold Metal Thread
Rajmahal Silver Metal Thread
Rajmahal Rajcord (silver)
Rajmahal Smooth Sadi Thread (silver)
Rajmahal Pearl Sadi Thread (gold)
Rajmahal Check Sadi Thread (gold)
Needles: Crewel 7, 9, 10.

Techniques
Couching, laid sadi, sadi beading.

Stitches
Backstitch, couching, fly stitch, French knots, Roumanian couching, satin stitch, split stitch, straight stitch, Turkey stitch.

Method
Prepare the fabric and transfer the design as usual.

Dragonfly

Work the tail first in long straight stitches using six strands of 805. Begin with the stitches on the outside edge of the tail. Add more stitches inside these, then more stitches towards the body.

The tail sections are marked with smooth sadi laid over the tail using two strands of 805 as the working thread.

The body is satin stitch in six strands of 805. Smooth sadi again marks the sections.

Six strands of 25 are used to work the satin stitch head. The eyes are worked

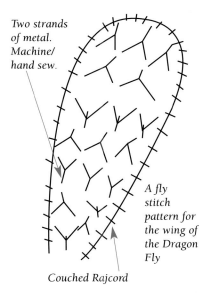

Two strands of metal. Machine/hand sew.

A fly stitch pattern for the wing of the Dragon Fly

Couched Rajcord

in French knots using two strands of 29 with two strands of silver metal thread.

The wings are outlined with Rajcord that is couched with two strands of silver metal thread. Interlocking fly stitches of two strands of silver metal thread make dainty wings.

The legs are straight stitches using one strand 805 and one strand 25 combined in one needle.

Ladybird

The ladybird is worked with single strands of thread and a Crewel 10 needle.

Work the legs in split stitch using one strand of 29.

With a single strand of 255, backstitch around the outline of the ladybird. These stitches must be very small. Embroider the body with one strand of 225 in satin stitch. The spots are satin stitch in 29.

The centre wing line is split stitch with one strand of 226.

The head is satin stitch, using 29. In the same shade, work French knots to form the eyes, then straight stitch for the feelers.

Bumble Bee

Use one strand of 311 to backstitch around the wings. These stitches must be very, very small. Fill in the wings with Roumanian couching, using one strand each of 101 and 311. The gold veins are metal thread. Pearl sadi is gently stretched and then couched with a single strand of gold metal thread to outline the wings.

Backstitch around the body using 93. Again, the stitches must be very, very small. The body is worked in Turkey stitch, using six strands of 93, 175 and 235. The diagram shows the placement of the colours.

The head is three strands of 175 in satin stitch.

The feelers and legs are two strands of 175. Two small pieces of check sadi are laid as beads, using 175, to highlight the body.

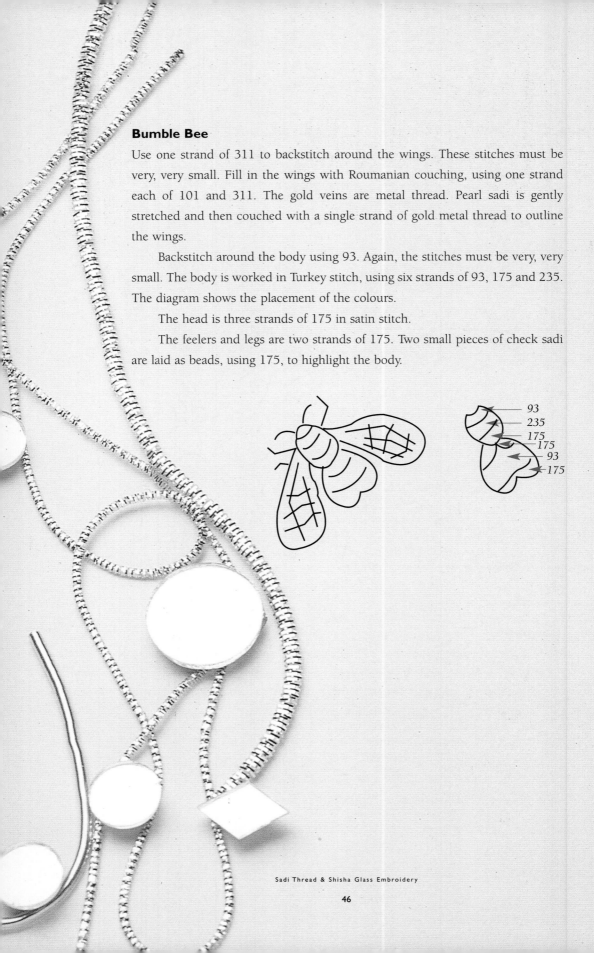

Sadi & Shisha 'R'

This design is meant as a guide to working letters of your choice. The techniques described below can, with a little modification, be applied to any letter of the alphabet. It may not always be suitable to use shisha

Materials
Rajmahal Gold Metal Thread
Rajmahal Rajcord (gold)
Rajmahal Smooth Sadi Thread (gold)
Rajmahal Check Sadi Thread (gold)
Rajmahal Pearl Sadi Thread (gold)
Rajmahal Shisha (Mirror) Glass (large round)
Rajmahal Shisha (Mirror) Glass (small diamond)
Yellow felt (light grey if you are using silver sadi)
Cotton to attach the felt.
Needles: Crewel 9, Straw 8.

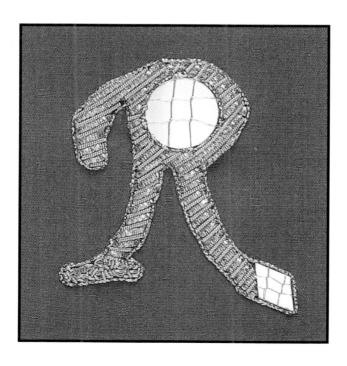

Techniques

Couching, basic shisha frame, laid sadi, sadi beading.

Stitches

Couching, stab stitch.

Method

Prepare the background fabric and transfer the design as usual.

Cut a piece of felt in the shape of the 'R' (or your chosen letter). Stab stitch the felt to the fabric around the outside edge only. This means that the inside edge of the 'R' will remain raised. If more prominence is required, cut out a narrower felt 'R' and stab stitch it to the fabric first. Then cover this with the felt 'R' in the finished size.

Attach the pieces of shisha with a basic shisha frame using gold metal thread.

All the sadi threads are stitched on with two strands of waxed metal thread. Pieces of pearl and check sadi are laid alternatively over the felt.

Small beads of smooth sadi feature on the base of the left-hand upright of the 'R'.

Rajcord is couched with metal thread all around the outline of the 'R'.

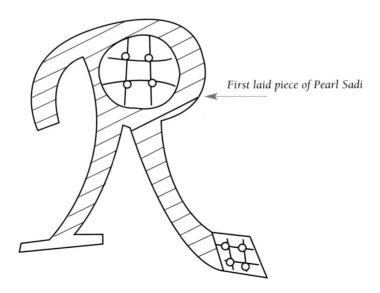

First laid piece of Pearl Sadi

A Sadi Sampler

Materials

Rajmahal Art Silk 44, 90, 133, 200, 201, 231, 371, 374.

Rajmahal Gold Metal Thread

Rajmahal Silver Metal Thread

Rajmahal Rajcord (gold & silver)

Rajmahal Check Sadi Thread (gold & silver)

Rajmahal Broad Check Sadi Thread (gold & silver)

Rajmahal Pearl Sadi Thread (gold & silver)

Rajmahal Smooth Sadi Thread (gold & silver)

Rajmahal Broad Smooth Sadi Thread (gold)

Felt (yellow)

Fibre Fill

Gold coloured cord $^1/_8$"(3 mm) diameter – about 20 in (50 cm)

Needles: Crewel 8, 9; Straw 8.

Techniques
Couching, sadi beading, laid sadi, sadi lazy daisy.

Stitches
Burden stitch, chain stitch, colonial knots, couching, fly stitch, French knots, lazy daisy stitch.

Method
1. Rows of stem stitch worked in the same direction, with three strands of 90. Attach gold broad smooth sadi in a radiating pattern, using laid sadi technique.
2. Form colonial knots using three strands of 200, and make a few knots using two strands of gold metal thread.
3. Stitch gold smooth sadi beads down with gold metal thread, and use three strands of 231 to work colonial knots.

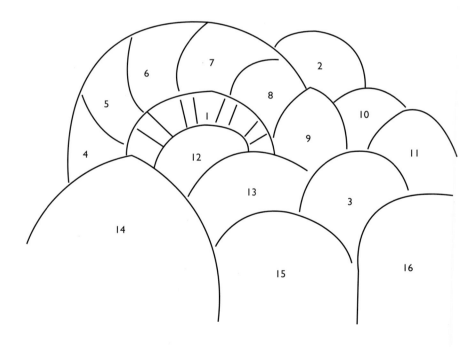

4. Gold smooth sadi, attached with gold metal thread, is used to form fly stitch.

5. Cut silver broad check sadi and gold broad check sadi as beads and stitch them down with one strand of gold metal thread.

6. The area is first padded with two layers of felt, held in place with stab stitches. A pattern of two rows of silver pearl sadi followed by one row of gold smooth sadi is repeated until the area is filled. Use two strands of waxed gold metal thread to couch the sadi.

7. Fibre fill is pushed under a piece of felt to obtain the raised effect, and the felt is then covered with a mixture of gold smooth, pearl and check sadi beads using two strands of 44 waxed.

8. Use silver Rajcord in lazy daisy stitch with silver smooth sadi lazy daisy centres. The working thread is silver metal thread.

9. Has been left unworked for design space.

10. Rows of gold pearl sadi couched with two strands of waxed gold metal thread.

11. Form gold pearl sadi and gold smooth sadi into chain stitches using gold metal thread.

12. Using three strands of 133, stitch a lattice design in straight stitches. Where the threads intersect, attach very small beads of gold smooth sadi.

13. Couch stretched gold pearl sadi with three strands of 133.

14. Gold and silver Rajcord couched over gold cord (see the photograph for where to place the cord and the Rajcord). French knots are worked with two strands of either 133, 371 or 374.

15. Diagonal rows of gold and silver broad check sadi couched with the appropriate metal threads.

16. Burden stitch over laid gold pearl sadi using six strands of 374.

Silhouette of a Rose

Materials

Rajmahal Art Silk 44
Rajmahal Gold Metal Thread
Rajmahal Rajcord (gold)
Rajmahal Check Sadi Thread (gold)
Rajmahal Smooth Sadi Thread (gold)
Rajmahal Broad Smooth Sadi Thread (gold)
Rajmahal Pearl Sadi Thread (gold)
Needles: Straw 8; Crewel 7, 9.

Techniques

Couching, sadi beading, laid sadi.

Stitches

Couching.

Method

Prepare the background fabric and transfer the design.

For the petals, cut pieces of broad smooth sadi to fit the tacking lines. Couch in place using six strands of 44.

Waxed metal thread (two strands) is used in all the following procedures.

Cut small pieces of check sadi and stitch them into place as beads to form the centre of the rose.

The stalk is two rows of couched pearl sadi.

The calyx is made of small chips of smooth and check sadi, stitched in the bead technique. Each side is a short length of pearl sadi applied in the laid technique.

The leaf is Rajcord, couched using one strand of metal thread.

The Fairies' Shisha Tree

Materials

Rajmahal Art Silk 45, 94, 111, 113, 131, 133, 141, 161, 181, 184, 231, 241, 788.

Rajmahal Gold Metal Thread

Rajmahal Silver Metal Thread

Rajmahal Rajcord (gold & silver)

Rajmahal Smooth Sadi Thread (gold & silver)

Rajmahal Check Sadi Thread (gold)

Rajmahal Broad Check Sadi Thread (silver)

Rajmahal Pearl Sadi Thread (gold & silver)

Rajmahal Shisha (Mirror) Glass (large round) – eighteen pieces

A copper washer

A fibre washer

Needles: Crewel 7, 9; Straw 8; Chenille 22.

Techniques

Basic shisha frame, triangle shisha frame, covered ring frame, five spoke foundation, needleweaving, couching, laid sadi, sadi beading.

Stitches

Buttonhole stitch, chain stitch, colonial knots, couching, double crochet, French knots, herringbone stitch (irregular), lazy daisy stitch, stab stitch, straight stitch.

Method

Prepare the background fabric and transfer the design.

The leaves are silver and gold smooth sadi threaded as for a bead and stitched into position with one strand of gold metal thread.

Gold pearl sadi – which has been stretched slightly then couched with two strands waxed gold metal thread – forms the trunk and branches.

Eighteen shisha flowers bloom on this tree! The flowers are worked as follows.

1. Make a five spoke foundation. Then decorate it with needleweaving in 113 by going over and under the spokes to form a spider web. Finish as for the

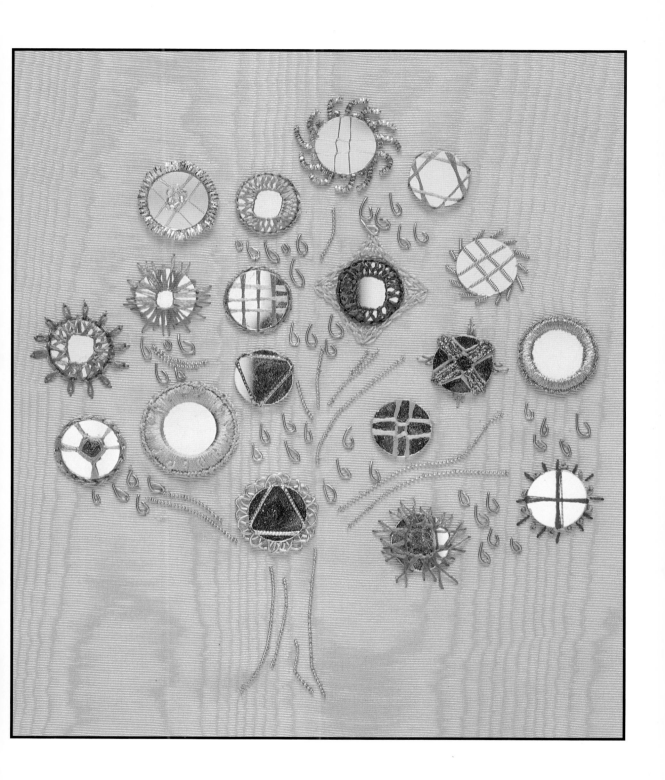

five spoke foundation. Chain stitch around the shisha using six strands of 111.

2. Straight stitches of four strands of 181 radiate from the centre of the basic shisha frame.

3. Decorate a basic shisha frame with buttonhole stitch worked with four strands of 241.

4. Use gold Rajcord to form a triangle shisha frame.

5. This is a typical Indian design, and uses three strands of 113 and 141. The star is rows of chain stitch, and the shisha is decorated with a buttonhole edge over a basic shisha frame.

6. Silver metal thread is crocheted around the copper washer. Place the washer over the shisha and stab stitch the edge of the crocheting to the fabric.

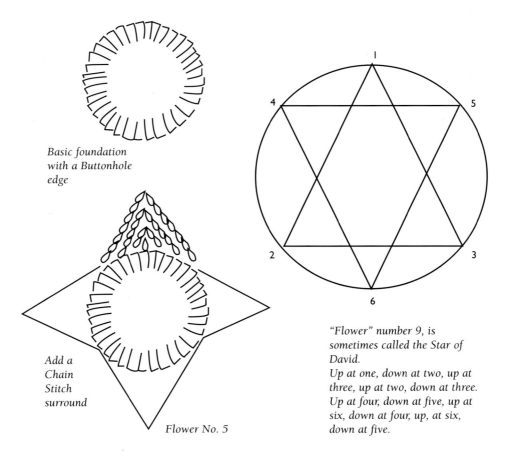

Basic foundation with a Buttonhole edge

Add a Chain Stitch surround

Flower No. 5

"Flower" number 9, is sometimes called the Star of David.
Up at one, down at two, up at three, up at two, down at three. Up at four, down at five, up at six, down at four, up, at six, down at five.

7. Form a cross-shaped frame (one vertical stitch and one horizontal stitch) with six strands of 184. Around the edge are straight stitches in the same colour. Use six strands of 45 to form French knots.

8. Double crochet around the fibre washer with six strands of 131. The covered washer is then stab stitched to the fabric using two strands of 131. The colonial knots are worked in six strands 231.

9. The shisha is held with six strands of 161 worked as a Star of David pattern (see drawing).

10. Work a basic shisha frame with six strands of 94.

11. Decorate a basic shisha frame with irregular herringbone stitch using 788.

12. Create a silver Rajcord triangle frame. Then, around the circumference of the shisha, add interlocking loops of silver smooth sadi, applied using the laid sadi technique.

13. Start with a basic shisha frame using two strands of gold metal thread, then apply gold check sadi in a spiral design using the laid sadi technique. The sadi is cut a little longer than the straight line between the stitching points, allowing the sadi to curve.

14. Silver metal thread is threaded through silver pearl sadi for the foundation. Add pieces of silver pearl sadi (treated as beads) around the outside.

15. A basic shisha frame in two strands of silver metal thread holds the shisha in place. A length of silver broad check sadi is couched into position around the shisha using silver metal thread. Smooth sadi beads are stitched around the centre of the basic frame.

16. This basic shisha frame has an open buttonhole edge, worked in six strands of 161. With three strands of 788, work a lazy daisy into each buttonhole loop. Using 788, embroider straight stitches from the outside to the centre frame.

17. The basic shisha frame is worked in 131. Four straight stitches in gold Rajcord, going under then over the central square of the frame, decorate between the basic frame stitches. Three straight stitches, the middle being longer, are worked from the edge of the shisha.

18. Three vertical and three horizontal stitches are worked in a lattice pattern over the shisha with six strands of 133. The same thread is used to stem stitch around the shisha.

Shisha with Covered Washers

Materials

Rajmahal Art Silk 165

Rajmahal Gold Metal Thread

Rajmahal Pearl Sadi Thread (gold)

Rajmahal Shisha (Mirror) Glass (large round)

1 small round Shisha (Mirror) glass

Washers: one $^{11}/_{12}$" (23 mm) diameter; and one $^{5}/_{8}$" (16 mm) diameter.

Crotchet hook

Felt (a small amount of yellow)

Needles: Crewel 8

Techniques

Couching.

Stitches

Crochet, stem stitch, stab stitch, whipped stem stitch.

Method

Prepare the background fabric and transfer the design as usual.

Crochet around the washers with the metal thread, packing the crocheting very tightly. Place the washers over the pieces of shisha, and stab stitch them to the fabric through the edge of the crocheting.

The stem to the large flower is pearl sadi, doubled over at the 'flower' end. Couch the sadi in place, keeping the stitches at right angles to the sadi, using gold metal thread.

The stem above the small shisha is a single length of pearl sadi couched with waxed gold metal thread.

The tendril is pearl sadi couched with two strands of 165.

The leaf is padded with two layers of felt. The slightly smaller felt layer is stitched in place first and then covered with the full sized piece. Beginning on the outside of the leaf, couch pearl sadi over the felt using two strands of 165.

Work a row of stem stitch beside the central and the small 'flower' stems in 165.

To finish your embroidery, work a row of stem stitch in two strands of 165, whipped with gold metal thread, as the ground for the 'flower' to grow from.

Shisha Tortoise

The Shisha Tortoise is fun to embroider.

Materials
Rajmahal Art Silk 101, 104, 171, 175, 311, 802, 805, 841.
Rajmahal Shisha (Mirror) Glass (large diamond) – 3 pieces
Rajmahal Shisha (Mirror) Glass (small diamond) – 9 pieces
Felt: fawn or light brown
Tulle: 6 in x 8" (15 cm x 20 cm) in light brown or tan
Needles: Crewel 7, 9.

Techniques
Fabric cover.

Stitches

Backstitch, French knots, satin stitch, stab stitch, straight stitch, split stitch.

Method

Make a pattern of the tortoise shell using tracing paper. Pin the pattern onto the felt, and cut it out.

Now cut a second shell shape approximately $^7/_{12}$" (1.5 cm) smaller in circumference than the first. Stab stitch the smaller felt shell to the background fabric. The stitches should lie at right angles to the edge of the felt. The stitching direction is from the outside inwards.

Place the larger felt shape over the smaller one, and attach it as before.

The pieces of shisha are held in place with a single piece of tulle. Cut the tulle about $1^1/_4$"(4 cm) larger than the shell, on all sides. Begin with the large pieces of shisha. Backstitch around each piece, close to the edge of the glass, using three strands of 104.

Place the smaller pieces of shisha as illustrated and backstitch around them in the same fashion.

Backstitch around the shell, on the background material, close to the felt, using small stitches. Cut the tulle around the backstitching.

Use long straight stitches of six strands in either 101, 104 or 171 (colour depends on your tulle and background fabric) to embroider the shell.

Work the legs in split stitch using one strand of 311 and one strand of 171, combined in the needle. Add a few French knots, over the split stitches, with two strands of 841.

The feet are embroidered in satin stitch using one strand each of 311 and 171, combined in one needle.

The head is worked in satin stitch using two strands of 171.

The lower jaw is satin stitch shaded with two strands of 311 and two strands of 171. The eye and outline are done in 175 in straight stitch.

The rock is a series of straight stitches with two strands of 175 and 101 combined in the needle.

The grass is one strand each of 802 and 805 worked together in straight stitches.

Blue Diamond Flower

Materials
Rajmahal Art Silk 122, 121, 421.
Rajmahal Gold Metal Thread
Rajmahal Check Sadi Thread (gold)
Rajmahal Pearl Sadi Thread (gold or silver)
Rajmahal Smooth Sadi Thread (gold)
Rajmahal Shisha (Mirror) Glass (large diamond). Three pieces
Rajmahal Shisha (Mirror) Glass (small diamond). Two pieces
Rajmahal Shisha (Mirror) Glass (small round). Two pieces
Felt (yellow)
Needles: Crewel 7, 8; Straw 8.

Techniques
Basic shisha frame, couching, sadi beading, laid sadi.

Stitches
Buttonhole stitch, chain stitch, straight stitch.

Method
Prepare for the embroidery as usual.

Attach the three large diamond shisha using four strands of 122. Use the basic shisha frame technique, plus an extra straight stitch across the narrow points.

Cut small lengths of check sadi to thread, like a bead, onto waxed 122. Take the needle under the central foundation threads out to the edge of the shisha, down through the material and up again, ready to attach the next piece of sadi. Repeat this process around the three diamonds.

Cut pieces of check sadi the length of the sides of the large diamond shisha. Attach them to the background fabric using the laid sadi technique. Add two couching stitches to each length of check sadi to hold the lengths in position.

The small round pieces of shisha are attached with three strands of waxed 121. After attaching the shisha with the basic shisha frame, buttonhole stitch around the lower half of each shisha. Using six strands of 421, chain stitch next

*Foundation
Stitches on
a Diamond*

to the buttonholing. Finish the other half of the circle as for the large diamonds.

The small diamonds are attached with the basic shisha frame using three strands of 421. Two rows of chain stitch using six strands of 421 surround the small diamonds.

Pad the centre of the large-diamond 'flower' with two pieces of felt – one smaller than the other. Stab stitch the pieces into place. Smooth sadi is cut into beads and stitched over the felt using gold metal thread. Be sure to cover all the felt. The idea is to have the sadi at different angles so as to catch as much light as possible. The central stem is pearl sadi cut and laid, using metal thread, to resemble stem stitch. Pearl sadi is couched, with metal thread, from the round small pieces of shisha to the stem.

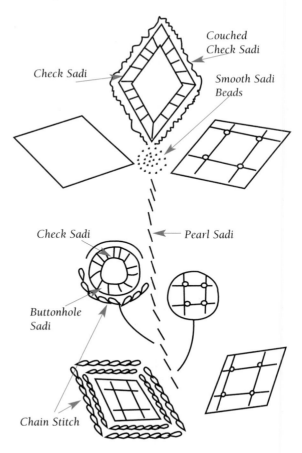

Golden Wattle

Materials

Rajmahal Art Silk 44, 126, 261, 264, 802, 805, 926.

Rajmahal Gold Metal Thread

Rajmahal Shisha (Mirror) Glass (small round) – twelve pieces

Needle: Crewel 9

Techniques

Basic shisha frame, couching.

Stitches

Backstitch, couching, French knots, satin stitch, split stitch, stem stitch, whipped stem stitch.

Method

The two outside leaves are embroidered in shaded satin stitch. The shading is achieved by working with two strands each of 802, 805 and 926 (in various combinations).

The veins are two strands of metal thread, couched with one strand of metal thread.

The turned-back section of the central leaf is worked in shaded split stitch using the same colours as mentioned above in two strands, but the stitch direction now becomes more vertical, and 802 the more prominent colour.

The other section of this leaf is in the shaded satin stitches of the outer leaves. A single strand of 126 in backstitch helps to visually define the folded underside of this leaf.

The stalks of the leaves are two rows of whipped stem stitch, using three strands of thread – one strand of 44 and two strands of 926 – combined in the same needle, then whipped with a strand of gold metal thread.

The wattle stems are worked in the same way, but with only one row of stem stitch.

To create the shisha wattle, work a basic shisha frame over each piece of shisha, using two strands of gold metal thread. The blossoms are made with straight stitches around the central foundation. Keep in mind that these stitches should appear to radiate from a central point. The surrounding French knots are single strands of 261 or 264.

The wattle bud is single strands of 261, 264 and 802 mixed together in the needle and made into French knots.

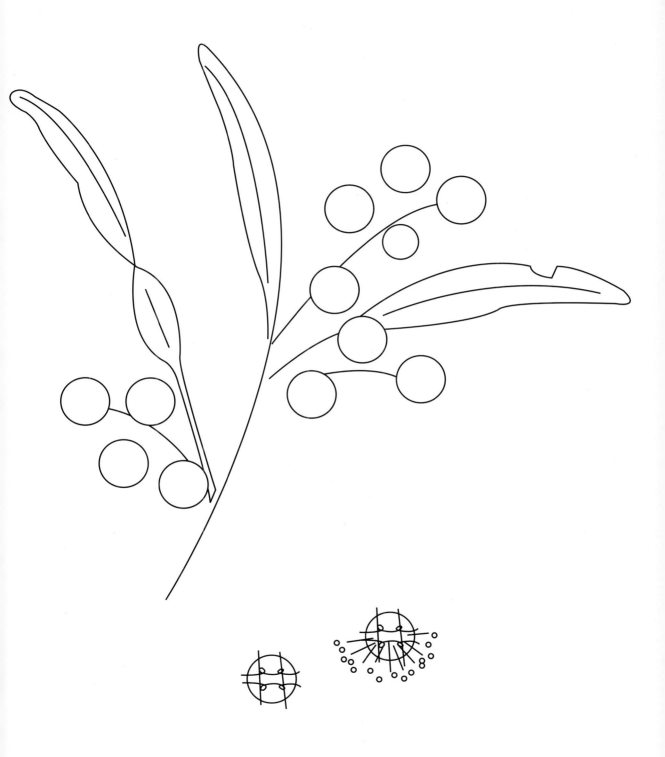

Sadi Wallflowers

Materials
Rajmahal Art Silk 111, 113, 115, 802, 805.
Rajmahal Gold Metal Thread
Rajmahal Rajcord (gold)
Rajmahal Smooth Sadi Thread (gold)
Rajmahal Check Sadi Thread (gold)
Rajmahal Pearl Sadi Thread (gold)
Needles: Crewel 7, 8, Straw 8.

Techniques
Couching, sadi bullion, sadi lazy daisy, laid sadi, sadi beading.

Stitches
Bullions, chain stitch, colonial knots, coral stitch, couching, lazy daisy stitch, stem stitch, Coral Knot Stitch.

Method
Prepare fabric and transfer
diagram in the usual way.

Embroider coral stitch in all flowers first before commencing the sadi embroidery. Three strands of thread are used unless otherwise stated.

Flower 1:   The markings in the petal are worked in coral stitch using 113. Check sadi is couched with metal thread along the petal outlines. Several small pieces of smooth sadi are stitched in the bead technique to indicate the flower centre.

Flower 2:   The coral stitch is worked with two strands of 113 and one strand of 115 combined in one needle. Rajcord is couched with metal thread in two parallel rows to form the petal outlines. Radiating out from the centre, four $^5/_{12}$" (1 cm) lengths of smooth sadi are stitched down in the laid technique. The centre of the flower is a piece of check sadi stitched down as a bead.

Flower 3: The coral stitch is worked in two strands of 115. The flower centre is a colonial knot worked in Rajcord. The petal outline is pearl sadi couched with gold metal thread. The four outer lazy daisy stitches are smooth sadi held in place with three couching stitches in gold metal thread. The inner lazy daisy stitches are worked in three strands of 113.

The stems are worked in chain stitch using six strands of 805.

Make some of the small flower centres in bullions and others in coral knot stitch, using four strands of thread in shades 111, 113 or 115 for variety and interest. Complete the outer petals with smooth sadi bullions. Stems and leaves are worked in three strands of 802 or 805 using stem stitch or lazy daisy stitch.

The Strawberry Plant

Materials

Rajmahal Art Silk 45, 65, 90, 152, 165, 255, 256, 421.

Rajmahal Gold Metal Thread

Rajmahal Shisha (Mirror) Glass (small round). One piece

Rajmahal Shisha (Mirror) Glass (small diamond). One piece

Covered Cake Wire 28

Fibre Fill (a small amount)

Cream cotton fabric (homespun or quilter's muslin)

Mid-blue cotton fabric (background fabric)

Silk organza (background fabric)

Vilene (medium weight, not the self-adhesive type)

Glue stick

Needles: Crewel 8, 9; Chenille 22

Techniques

Couching, basic shisha frame.

Stitches

Buttonhole stitch, chain stitch, colonial knots, couching, detached buttonhole stitch, French knots, stab stitch, stem stitch, split stitch, straight stitch.

Method

Preparing slips

The petals of the strawberry flower, the strawberry and the bud calyxes are worked as slips and then attached to the design.

Trace or draw the strawberry flower petals onto a piece of cream cotton fabric. Mount the

cotton into a frame. Using one strand of 90, couch the cake wire around the outline of each petal. Try to have the ends of the wire approximately equal lengths and pointing to the outside of the frame (see diagram). Work about 12 couching stitches per petal.

Using one strand of 90, cover the cake wire completely with buttonhole stitches. On the outer edge of the petal the stitches must be very close to the wire, but the 'legs' of the buttonhole stitch are longer and face toward the centre of the petal. Then, work small chain stitches over the buttonhole stitch 'legs', up against the inside of the wire.

The petals are then embroidered in shaded split stitch, taking care to cover the chain stitch. Use two strands of 90 at the outside of the petal, and one strand each of 90 and 421 towards the centre of the flower. After the embroidery is completed, carefully cut the petals close to the buttonhole edge.

Trace or draw the strawberry and the bud calyx onto Vilene, and mount the Vilene in a frame. With one strand each of 165 and 152 (in the same needle), work very small buttonhole stitches around the edge of the calyx. The same threads are used to fill in with split stitch. Cut out the calyx very close to the buttonhole edge.

The main design

The background fabric for this embroidery is mid-blue cotton under silk organza. Care must be taken to match the grain of the two materials before they are stitched together around the edges. The design is then applied in the usual way.

The strawberry is worked in detached buttonhole stitch using two strands of thread. It is easier to work the detached buttonhole with the fabric over your finger rather than in a frame. The top half of the strawberry is stitched with two strands of 255, blending into one strand each of 255 and 256 (combined in the needle) for the centre section. Use two strands of 256 for the lower section. Both the strawberry and leaves will be padded, so do not complete all the detached buttonhole until after padding.

The three leaves are worked in detached buttonhole stitch. The top sections are worked in two strands of 165, then one strand each of 65 and 165 (combined in the needle), finishing with two strands of 65 for the rows closest to the stalks.

When you still have several rows of detached buttonhole to complete, pad the strawberry and the leaves by gently pushing small pieces of Fibre Fill under the buttonhole stitches with the blunt end of a large-eyed needle. Don't over pad or the background fabric may buckle. After padding, finish the last rows of detached buttonhole to complete the leaves and the strawberry. Stab stitch the last rows closed to enclose the padding.

Finish the leaves by outlining them with stem stitch using two strands of metal thread. The veins are one strand of metal thread in straight stitch. Complete the strawberry by outlining it with two strands of 255 combined with one strand of metal thread, using stem stitch. Work a few French knots in metal thread on the strawberry.

The stalks are worked in stem stitch using two strands of 421 combined in the needle with one strand 165.

To make the centre of the strawberry flower, attach the round shisha using a basic shisha frame with three strands of 421. Buttonhole stitch around the inside centre square of the frame. Chain stitch around the circumference of the shisha using three strands of 421. Still using three strands of 421, buttonhole stitch twice into each chain. Work another round, buttonholing twice into the previous loop. With two strands of 45, work colonial knots around the buttonhole edge.

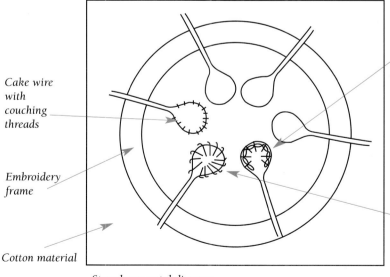

Cake wire with couching threads

Embroidery frame

Cotton material

Small Chain stitches over the Buttonhole "legs", stitched next to the wire on the inside of the petal.

Very close Buttonhole stitches next to the outside of the wire. The long legs of the Buttonhole stitch towards the centre of the petal.

Strawberry petal diagram

The diamond shisha is attached with three strands of 421 using a basic shisha frame. Outline with chain stitch using 421 and work colonial knots over the chain stitch with two strands metal thread.

Stab stitch both the calyx into place with one strand of 421.

Finish the strawberry flower by attaching the petals, as follows, one at a time. Take a large needle and making a hole in the fabric at the point where the base of the petal will sit. Pass the 'tail' wires of a petal through to the wrong side of the fabric. Repeat with an opposite petal. On the wrong side of the fabric, oversew the four pieces of wire together and catch them to the material with a few stitches under the shisha. The remaining two pairs of petals are finished in the same way. Cut the wires ³/₄i" (2 cm) from where they were pulled through the material.

Cut a circle of the blue background cotton material 1³/₈" (3.5 cm) in diameter, and apply a small amount of glue (use only 'stick' glue) to the circle. Press the glued fabric onto the wires (making sure that the glue comes into contact with the wires only) by running your finger up and down each pair of wires (see drawing). Leave to dry, preferably overnight.

Between each petal, work three straight stitches using two strands of 421 and one strand of gold metal thread combined in the needle.

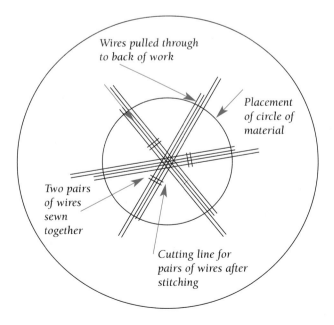

Wires pulled through to back of work

Placement of circle of material

Two pairs of wires sewn together

Cutting line for pairs of wires after stitching

Raised Pink Bell Flowers

Materials

Rajmahal Art Silk 200, 261, 311, 421, 521, 742, 745.

Rajmahal Shisha (Mirror) Glass (small round). Four pieces

Rajmahal Shisha (Mirror) Glass (large round). Two pieces

Cotton fabric (homespun or quilter's muslin) 9" x 13" (22 cm x 33 cm) if using an oval frame or 11" (28 cm) square if using a round frame.

Vilene (medium weight iron-on) 7" x 14" (18 cm x 36 cm)

Pellon or fine batting

Covered Cake Wire 28

Needles: Crewel 7, 8; Tapestry 24; Chenille 22.

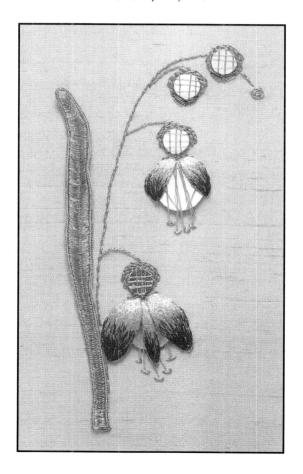

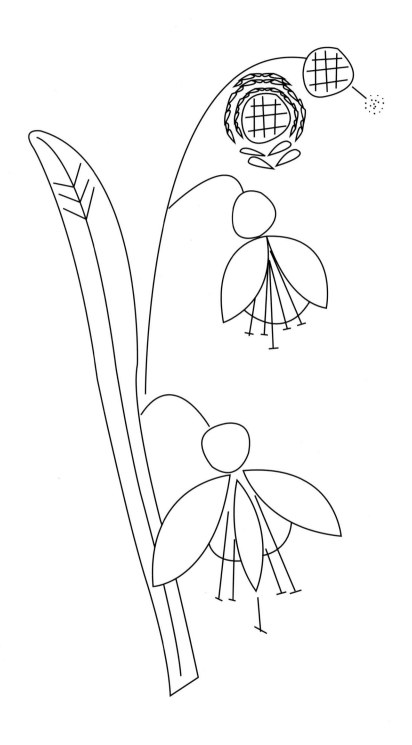

Techniques
Basic shisha frame, triangle shisha frame.

Stitches
Buttonhole stitch, chain stitch, fly stitch, lazy daisy, split stitch, stem stitch, straight stitch, whipped stem stitch.

Method
Prepare the background fabric and transfer the design in the usual way.

Preparing slips
Draw or trace the five petals onto iron-on Vilene. You require two pieces of Vilene approximately 7" (18 cm) square, pressed together. The petals must be worked in a frame.Using a single strand of 742, work small, close buttonhole stitches around the edges. Chain stitch over the buttonhole 'legs', i.e. the straight part of the buttonhole stitch.

The filling shading is embroidered in split stitch using two strands of thread. An approximate guide to the shading is:

- tips of the petals, two strands of 745;
- moving through to 745 and 742 (which can be stitched both in one strand of each and as separate colours);
- then two strands of 742;
- then a small area blending 742 with 200;
- finally the top section of the petals is two strands of 200;
- cut out the petals close to the buttonholing.

The petals are now 'reverse padded'. This is a technique I have developed when a smooth padding is required. It is very simple! Cut pellon or fine batting to the shape of each petal, but slightly smaller. Slip stitch the padding into place on the wrong side of the fabric, making sure the stitches go through the back of the stitching threads and not through the fabric.

Trace the leaf onto the cotton fabric, and place the fabric in a frame. Working with one strand of 521, couch the cake wire in place over the outline of the leaf. Using the same thread, buttonhole over the wire taking very small, close stitches. Keeping close to the wire on the outside, stitch the 'legs' of the buttonhole stitch towards the vein of the leaf, making them uneven lengths.

Chain stitch over the legs of the buttonhole stitch, close to the inside of the wire using 521. The leaf is embroidered in fly stitch, shading in three strands and using various combinations of 521, 421, 261 and 311. Cut out the leaf close to the buttonhole edge.

Main design

Attach four small shisha, to form the flower buds and calyxes, by using a variation on the basic shisha frame technique. Working with two strands of 421, make three horizontal and three vertical stitches across the shisha, weaving the vertical stitches under and over the horizontal stitches.

Using three strands of 521, chain stitch around the circumference of each shisha. Chain stitch around all but the lower third of each shisha with two more parallel rows. Use one strand each of 742 and 745 (combined in the needle) to embroider lazy daisy stitches below the buds.

Two small shisha 'calyxes' sit atop the flowers. Stitch a line of four horizontal chain stitches to link the calyxes to the flowers, using two strands of 421.

The two large shisha are attached by a triangle shisha frame using three strands of 742. The point of the triangle is at the base of the petals.

The stamens are worked in long straight stitches using three strands of 742 for the vertical stitches and three strands of 311 for the small horizontal straight stitches For the main stem, use one strand each of 421, 521 and 311 in whipped stem stitch. The small stems are stem stitched using one strand each of 421 and 521 (combined in the needle).

The leaf is held in place by taking tiny stitches through the vein with one strand of 421. Work from the base of the leaf towards the tip. Leave the last $^3/_4$" (1.5cm) of the central vein unsecured to give life-like lift. Take the cake wire to the wrong side of the work and oversew the tail wires to the fabric under the leaf.

The tiny bud is embroidered with small straight stitches using one strand each of 261 and 421 (combined in the same needle).

Use one strand of 742 to stitch the petals into position.

Silvery Moon Owl

The owl is a challenge, but terrific fun to embroider!

Materials

Rajmahal Art Silk 25, 90, 96, 101, 126, 171, 173, 221, 841.

Rajmahal Silver Metal Thread

Rajmahal Rajcord (silver)

Rajmahal Shisha (Mirror) Glass (small round). Two pieces

Vilene (medium weight iron-on) two 7" (18 cm) square pieces

Covered Cake Wire 28

Cream cotton fabric 7" (18 cm) square

Fibre Fill (a small amount)

Tweezers

Needles: Tapestry 24; Chenille 22; Crewel 8, 9.

Techniques
Basic shisha frame

Stitches
Backstitch, buttonhole stitch, chain stitch, couching, fly stitch, French knots, Roumanian couching, satin stitch, stab stitch, straight stitch, stem stitch.

Method
The feathered look of the shaded areas is achieved by stitching in Roumanian couching.

Prepare your fabric and transfer the design as usual. A frame is absolutely essential when working this design – please, don't even attempt it without one!

Two strands of thread are used throughout unless otherwise stated.

Preparing slips
Cut the Vilene to fit your small embroidery frame. Trace the body of the owl onto one piece of Vilene and then iron the two adhesive sides together. Place the fused Vilene into a frame.

With one strand of 171, buttonhole stitch around the edge of the body. The stitches need to be small and close together. Shade the body with two-strand combinations of 171, 90 and 841 using Roumanian couching. The shading should be darkest towards the head. Trim very close to the buttonholed edge.

Trace the lower section of wing feathers onto cream coloured cotton. Leaving about 1 1/4" (3 cm) of wire at each end of the wing. If necessary, use tweezers to help bend the wire into shape before stitching. Couch the cake wire into place along the lower edge of the wing feathers using one strand of 90.

Buttonhole over the wire with one strand of 90. The stitches need to be very close to the outside of the wire and worked in uneven lengths towards the centre of each wing. Chain stitch close to the wire, over the buttonhole stitch 'legs' (i.e. the straight threads of the buttonhole stitch).

Use 90, 101 and 171 in various combinations of shaded satin stitch to fill the wings, keeping the wing tips pale. Emphasize the separation between the wing feathers with two vertical straight stitches in one strand of 173.

The small markings (that look like horizontal parallel bands) are actually small vertical straight stitches worked in one strand each of 173 and metal thread combined.

Trim very close to the buttonhole edge of the wings. Leave $^1/_5$" (5 mm) of cotton fabric along the top edge of the wing. Later this unembroidered edge will be stitched to the background fabric, and the cord of the upper wing couched over the top.

Main design

The wing feather nearest the body is embroidered directly onto the background fabric. Couch cake wire along the lower edge. Buttonhole over the wire using one strand of 90. The filling is one strand each of 90 and 221 (combined in one needle), adding occasional straight stitches in one strand of 171. Take the wire through to the back and secure where the wing and the body will be positioned.

Embroider the tail directly onto the background fabric using one strand each of 90 and171 combined in one needle. Roumanian stitch is used here. The tail markings are worked in fly stitch using one strand of 173 combined in one needle with one strand of metal thread.

Stitch the wings into place along the top edge and at the sides of the end feathers. Do not catch down the lower edges of the feathers. They will look far more natural if they are allowed to lift slightly from the fabric. Take the wires to the back of the fabric. Trim them to $^7/_{12}$" (1.5 cm) and catch them to the fabric behind the wings with a few small stitches.

To make the upper wing, use one strand of metal thread to couch Rajcord along the outer edges of the wing band. A double row of Rajcord is couched inside the first row of Rajcord. On the wrong side of the fabric, catch the ends of the Rajcord under the head area. Thread a tapestry needle with two strands of 171 and work fly stitches, both individually and in pairs, over sections of the upper wings.

Stab stitch the body into place, leaving the lower section open to allow for padding. Use the blunt end of a large-eyed needle to gently push small pieces of Fibre Fill underneath the body. Do not overfill the body with padding or the background fabric will become distorted. Use small stab stitches to close the lower body.

Embroider the head with one strand each of 101 and 171. Backstitch a heart-shaped outline around the face, then fill using two strands of 90 and one strand of 96 in the same needle in Roumanian couching.

Across the top of the heart-shaped face, work eleven French knots using three strands of 96. The triangular beak is worked in straight stitch using three strands of 25.

The Owl's Eyes

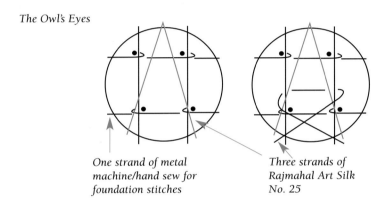

*One strand of metal
machine/hand sew for
foundation stitches*

*Three strands of
Rajmahal Art Silk
No. 25*

Attach the shisha eyes with a basic shisha frame and one strand of metal thread.

Use a Tapestry 24 needle with three strands of 25, to highlight the eyes (see drawing).

Outline the owl's body and head with one strand of 126 in small backstitches.

Outline the moon with one strand of metal thread in backstitch. The crescent is two strands of metal thread in rows of stem stitch.

The stars are comprised of four intersecting straight stitches

Stitch Guide

Stitch Guide

1. Backstitch
2. Buttonhole stitch
3. Detached Buttonhole stitch
4. Bullion stitch
5. Burden stitch
6. Twisted Chain stitch
7. Chain stitch
8. Couching
9. Cretan stitch
10. Colonial knot
11. Coral stitch
12. Crocheting
13. Crocheting (double)
14. Fly stitch
15. Coral Knot stitch
16. Lazy Daisy stitch
17. French Knot
18. Stab stitch
19. Herringbone stitch
20. Satin stitch
21. Roumanian Couching
22. Stem stitch
23. Whipped Stem stitch
24. Spider web stitch
25. Split stitch
26. Straight stitch
27. Turkey stitch

Back stitch

Buttonhole stitch

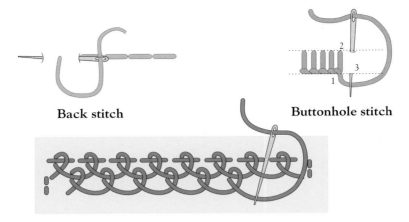

Detached buttonhole stitch

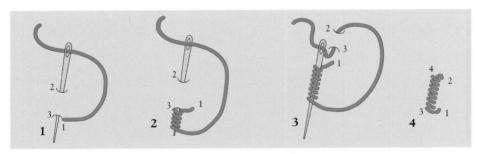

Bullion stitch

Burden stitch

Twisted chain stitch

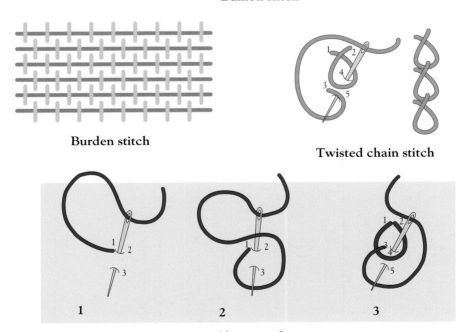

Chain stitch

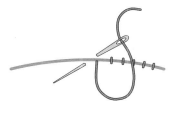

Couching

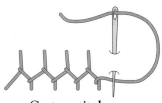

Cretan stitch

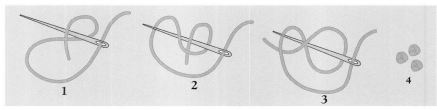

Colonial knot

1   2   3   4

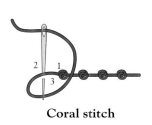

Coral stitch

Crocheting

Crocheting (double)

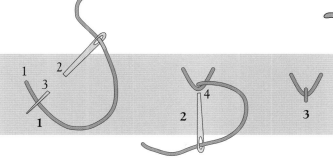

Fly stitch

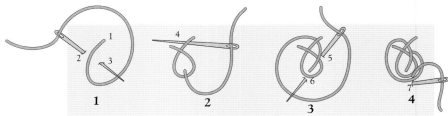

Coral knot stitch

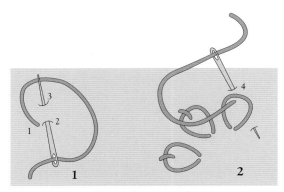

Lazy daisy stitch

1   2

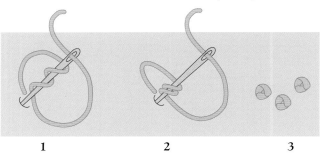

1   2   3

French knot

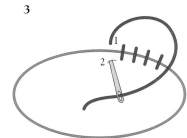

Stab stitch

Herringbone stitch

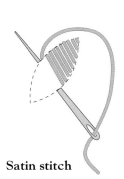

Satin stitch   **Roumanian couching**

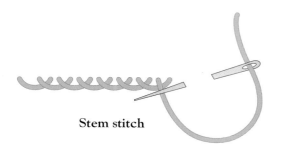

Stem stitch

Whipped stem stitch

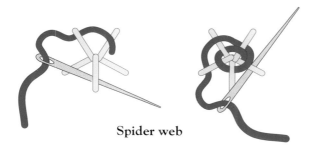

Spider web

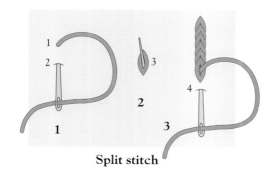

Split stitch

Straight stitch

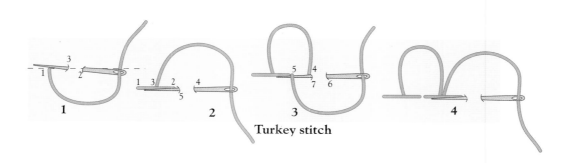

1 **2** **3** **4**

Turkey stitch

Betty Luke

Betty Luke was born in Tasmania and spent her early childhood in Boort, but the Victorian city of Bendigo has been her home for many years. With her husband Bill, she has six children and eight adorable grandchildren.

Needles and threads have never been far from Betty's hands; having completed her first piece of embroidery and a knitted jumper at the age of ten. Betty has been a member of the Victorian Embroiderers' Guild for many years and has been Secretary and Chairman of the Bendigo Branch of the Guild. Betty is a bobbin lace maker and a member of both the English Lace Guild and the Needlework Tool Society of Australia. For 20 years, she has been conserving and restoring textiles for the Golden Dragon Museum, Bendigo. In 1994, Betty graduated from Deakin University's course Art and Design for Embroiderers.

For your nearest stockist or distributor contact:

Rajmahal
1 Anderson Street
Bendigo Vic 3550
AUSTRALIA
Tel: +61 (03) 5441 7787
Fax: + 61 (03) 5441 7959
www.rajmahal.com.au